THE WEATHER CAT

Helen Cresswell

Illustrated by Barbara Walker

COLLINS

It was the school holidays.
Naomi and Otis were upstairs, helping their mother to make beds.
They heard a noise downstairs.
"There's someone downstairs," said Naomi.
"In the kitchen."

"Go down and see," her mum said.
"It will be Mr Briggs. I'll be down in a minute."

Naomi went downstairs and into the kitchen. There, rolling a reel of cotton across the floor, was a small tabby cat.

Naomi looked at the cat.
The cat looked back at Naomi.
"Hello, Mr Briggs!" said Naomi.
"Mum says she'll be down in a minute."
The tabby cat went back to its game and the cotton reel went to and fro.
Then Naomi gave it a kick.
The cat liked that. His tail twitched.
He crouched and sprang.

Naomi's mum came in.
"What's this?" said her mum.
"Mr Briggs and I are having a game of football,"
Naomi told her.
"He's good at it!"
Now Otis came in, too.
"That's not Mr Briggs!" he said.
"Yes it is," Naomi told him. "Another
Mr Briggs."

Naomi fetched a jug and a saucer.
"Would you like some milk, Mr Briggs?"
she asked.
"It's half time!"
The cat purred.
"You see," said Naomi. "It *is* his name!"

Just then the real Mr Briggs came in.
He had come to put in a new window pane.
"What's this?" he asked.
"I didn't know you had a cat."
"We didn't have one yesterday," Naomi told
him, "but today we have. His name is Mr Briggs.
Same as you."
"Fancy that!" said Mr Briggs.

At dinner time one Mr Briggs went home.
The other stayed, and ate fish tails and drank two saucers of milk.
You can guess which did which.

One Mr Briggs stayed all afternoon.
He curled himself up on the window sill.
He was still there when Dad came home.
"Can he stay?" Naomi asked.
"I think he likes it here," said Otis.
"If he did have a home already, he'd go there, I suppose," said Mum.
"He can stay if he likes," said Dad.

Mr Briggs did like.
The next day Naomi found an old white plate and a white dish.
Round the rim she painted the name Mr Briggs in black paint.
Now Mr Briggs had really come to stay.

Every morning Naomi came down and let him out.
Mr Briggs would drink a saucer of milk, and then go out into the yard.
After a week or two, Naomi began to notice something.

If it was fine, Mr Briggs would go and lie on top of the shed.
He was looking for birds.

If it was fine but cold, he would lie inside the shed.
He lay very still behind the sweeping brush.
He was looking for mice and spiders.

But if it was wet, Mr Briggs would soon come back into the house.
He came in on tip-toe, so as not to get his feet wet. Then he went into the cupboard under the stairs and slept all morning.

Then Naomi noticed something else.
On some days Mr Briggs would come and lie in his cupboard even when it was fine.
On the days when he did that, it always *did* rain, later on.

"Mr Briggs is a weather cat!" Naomi told her mum one day.
"He always knows when it's going to rain."
Mum was busy hanging out the washing.
"It isn't going to rain today," she said.
"Yes it is," Otis told her. "Mr Briggs is under the stairs."

Their mum laughed and went back inside.
Not long after, it began to rain. It poured.
Everyone ran out to take in the washing.
"I told you!" Naomi cried. "Mr Briggs is a weather cat!"

After that, they all took notice of what Mr Briggs did.
"He's on top of the shed today," Naomi's dad would say.
"No need to take my umbrella to work!"
Or "He's inside the shed – better wrap up warm!"

The family would wait to see what Mr Briggs did every morning.
If he lay on top of the shed, Mum had a wash day.

But if he went into his cupboard, she said, "Better wait till tomorrow. Mr Briggs is under the stairs."

One Saturday it was very fine weather, but
Mr Briggs went under the stairs.
"That's funny!" Naomi said.
"It doesn't look a bit like rain."
"There'll be no washing today," said her dad.
"Mr Briggs is never wrong."

At dinner time Mr Briggs was still in his cupboard. And there hadn't been a drop of rain. Not a single drop.
Naomi and Otis went and looked under the stairs. There lay Mr Briggs looking up at them.

And there, at his side, lay one, two, three, four little kittens.
"Mum! Dad!" yelled the children.
"Come and look!"

Mum and Dad ran to look in the cupboard.

Now the tabby cat is called Mrs Briggs, and has four weather kittens.
On fine days they lie on the roof of the shed, looking for birds.

On cold days they lie inside the shed, looking for mice and spiders.
And on wet days, they sleep in the cupboard under the stairs.

Soon Naomi and Otis will be giving the kittens away.
Does anyone want a weather cat?